EVANGELISM
For Every Day

**A 4-week course to help adults share their
faith in everyday situations**

BY STEPHEN PAROLINI

Loveland, Colorado

Group's
Apply·It·To·Life™
— ADULT BIBLE SERIES —

Group®

Evangelism For Every Day
Copyright © 1993 Group Publishing, Inc.

First Printing

Credits
Edited by Joani Schultz
Cover designed by Liz Howe
Cover photography by David Priest
Interior designed by Lisa Smith
Illustrations by RoseAnne Buerge

ISBN 1-55945-298-6
Printed in the United States of America

Contents

LESSON 1   11
Know What You Believe

Help adults learn that, before they share their faith with others, they must know what they believe—and what they don't yet understand.

LESSON 2   21
The Voice of Experience

Help adults discover that it's important to speak from experience and in plain language when telling someone about Christ.

LESSON 3   29
Actions Speak Louder

Help adults learn how their actions can be a powerful witness for Christ.

LESSON 4   37
I'll Do It My Way

Help adults discover how they can each use their unique gifts and abilities to fulfill Christ's great commission to teach the nations.

BONUS IDEAS   47

Introduction

EVANGELISM FOR EVERY DAY

- As much as 85 percent of church growth is made up of people who are simply changing churches.
- Only 32 percent of Americans today believe the Bible is true (as opposed to 65 percent in the 1960s).

Today's world is in desperate need of a Savior.

And it's our job to reach out to the world with the message that Christ died for us and that God loves us.

But the days of street-corner and tent-meeting evangelism are waning, and Christians are looking for new ways to share their faith. Not everyone can preach the gospel to millions the way Billy Graham has. Nor are most Christians called into professional ministry.

So how do we do it? How do regular, everday people teach the masses about Christ? We become evangelists for every day.

When Christ gave the great commission to his disciples in Matthew 28:18-20, he also gave their successors the same command and encouragement—to share God's love with the world. Well, we're the successors, and it's our job to tell others about God's love.

By focusing on what we know about God's love and what we don't yet understand about faith, we can effectively speak to others about Christ's sacrifice on the cross. When we speak in language that's free of the "Christianese" that confuses non-Christians (and separates churches), we can help others understand some of the mysteries of faith. And when we pattern our lives after Christ's, our actions can speak loudly about what it means to be a Christian.

This course will help adults discover ways to be evangelists in everyday situations—at work, at home, and among strangers. It will help them see that preaching from a soapbox, traveling door to door with the "Four Spiritual Laws," and handing out tracts in shopping centers aren't the only ways to spread the gospel. And it will help them uncover how they can use their unique gifts to reach others with God's love.

WHO IS THIS COURSE FOR?

Use *Evangelism For Every Day* with
- Sunday school classes,
- home study groups,
- weekday Bible study groups,
- men's Bible studies,
- women's Bible studies, and
- family classes.

WHAT WILL ADULTS LEARN?

During this course, adults will
- explore their personal beliefs on significant theological issues,
- determine what's important to know about their faith when telling others about Christ,
- discover the importance of speaking plainly about their faith,
- learn how their actions can be a powerful witness for Christ,
- examine their gifts and abilities, and
- learn how they can follow Christ's command to share the gospel.

WHAT IS ADULT EDUCATION?

To some, adult education means reading a book by a well-known Christian writer and discussing it in the company of friends. To others, it means sipping coffee while listening to an expert explain the root meaning of a Greek word and how it applies to a particular passage.

But adult education is much more—it's a road to discovery of the practical application of the Scriptures. It's an adventure into grace, faith, love, hope, fear, and salvation. And it's a journey that's embarked upon in community with others.

To this end, we have created a curriculum that will encourage adults to
- discover from each other's experience how to grow closer to God,
- dig into the Scriptures and come away with a personal application of the passages,
- explore how God works through relationships, and
- learn what it means to be a Christian in a non-Christian world.

Apply-It-to-Life Adult Bible Series™ is designed to help you facilitate powerful lessons to help adults grow in faith. Read on to find out how…

WHAT IS APPLY-IT-TO-LIFE ADULT BIBLE SERIES?

Think back on an important lesson you've learned in life. Did you learn it from reading about it? from hearing about it? from something you experienced? Chances are, the most important lessons you've learned came from something you experienced. That's what we call *active learning*—learning by doing. And active learning is a key element in Group's Apply-It-to-Life Adult Bible Series.

Another key element in this curriculum is something we call interactive learning. Interactive learning is a fancy name for learning through small-group interaction and discussion. While it may seem a simple enough concept, it's radically new to many churches that have stuck with the old standby, lectures, for so long. With interactive learning, each adult is actively engaged in discovering God's truth through interchange with other people and exploration of the Bible.

TIPS FOR A SUCCESSFUL ADULT CLASS

Here are seven tips for making Group's Apply-It-to-Life Adult Bible Series a success with your class.

ABOUT THE QUESTIONS AND ANSWERS…

The answers given after discussion questions are responses participants *might* give. They aren't the only answers or the "right" answers. If needed, use them to spark discussion. Real life doesn't always allow us to give the "right" answers. That's why some of the responses given are negative or controversial. If someone responds negatively, don't be shocked. Accept the person and use the opportunity to explore other angles of the issue.

To get more out of your discussions, use follow-up questions such as
- Tell me more…
- What do you mean by that?
- What makes you feel that way?

1. Be a facilitator, not a lecturer. Apply-It-to-Life Adult Bible Series is student-based, rather than teacher-based. Your job is to direct the activities and facilitate the discussions. Instead of being the "star" or the one who does all the talking, you become a choreographer of sorts—someone who gets everyone else involved in the discussion.

2. Teach adults how to form small groups. If the non-lecture concept is new to your class, help adults discover the benefits of small-group discussions by helping them form groups of four, three, or two—whatever the activity calls for. Small-group sharing allows for more discussion and involvement by all participants. It's not as threatening or scary to open up to two people as it would be to 20 or 200!

Some leaders decide not to break into groups because they want to hear everybody's ideas. Although their intentions are good, this method just doesn't work as well in eliciting full participation. Use a "report back" time after small groups talk to glean the best of the discussions for everyone.

3. Encourage relationship building. George Barna, in his insightful book about the church, *The Frog in the Kettle,* explains that adults today have a strong need to develop friendships. In a high-tech society of computers and lonely commutes, adults long for positive people contact. The church can be the place for that. Help adults form friendships through your class. What's discovered in the formal classroom setting will be better applied when friends support each other outside the classroom. Encourage relationship building.

4. Be flexible. Sometimes your class will complete every activity in the lesson with great success and wonderful learning. But what do you do if people go off on a tangent? or get stuck in one of the activities? What if you don't have time to finish the lesson?

Don't fret. The best learning takes place when adults are interested and engaged in meaningful discussion. And, when they move at their own pace. Because of the way this curriculum is designed, adults will discover the point of the whole lesson even if they get through only one activity. Relax...it's OK if you don't get everything done in one lesson.

5. Expect the unexpected. Active learning is an adventure that doesn't always take you where you think you're going. Don't be surprised if your lessons don't go exactly the way you planned them. Be open to the direction of the Holy Spirit. Take advantage of the teachable moments that come your way—they're some of the best opportunities for learning!

6. Participate—and encourage participation. Apply-It-to-Life Adult Bible Series is only as interactive as the people make it. Learning arrives out of dialogue. People need to grapple with and verbalize their questions and discoveries. Jump into discussions yourself. Use the possible responses after each question to spark further discussion in small groups if people seem stumped. You may feel like a cheerleader at times, but your efforts will be worth it. The more that people participate, the more they'll discover God's truths.

7. Trust the Holy Spirit. God sent the Holy Spirit as our helper. As you facilitate this curriculum, ask the Holy Spirit to help you facilitate the lessons. And ask the Holy Spirit to direct your class toward God's truth. Trust that God's Spirit can work through each person's discoveries—not just the teacher's.

WHAT ARE THE ELEMENTS OF APPLY-IT-TO-LIFE ADULT BIBLE SERIES?

The **Welcome** maps out the lesson's agenda. Adults like to know where you're headed and what to expect in the class.

The **Community Builder** helps your class members get to know each other. Meeting only once or twice a week provides barely enough time to learn each other's names, let alone feel comfortable with a group of adults. The Community Builder helps you create time for important relationships to build and grow.

The **Bible Exploration and Application** activities are designed to help adults discover how the Bible connects with the topic and how the lesson's point applies to their lives. It's in these varied activities that adults find answers to the "So what?" question. Through active- and interactive-learning methods, adults will find relevance in the Scriptures and commit to grow closer to God.

The **Closing** funnels the lesson's message into a time of creative reflection and prayer.

When you put all the sections together, you get a lesson that's fun and easy to teach. Plus, participants will get messages they'll remember and apply to their daily lives.

HOW TO USE THIS COURSE

BEFORE THE 4-WEEK SESSION

• Read the Introduction (p. 4) and review Tips for a Successful Adult Class (p. 5) and This Course at a Glance (p. 8).

• Decide how you'll publicize the course using the art on the Publicity Page (p. 9). Prepare fliers, newsletter articles, and posters as needed.

• Look at the Bonus Ideas (pp. 47-48) and decide which ones you'll use.

BEFORE EACH LESSON

• Read the opening statements, Objectives, and Bible Basis for the lesson. The Bible Basis shows how specific passages relate to adults today.

• Choose which activities you'll use from the lesson. Remember, it's not important to do every activity—choose the ones that best fit your group and time allotment.

• Gather necessary supplies from This Lesson at a Glance.

• Read each section of the lesson. Adjust where necessary for your class size and meeting room.

THIS COURSE AT A GLANCE

Before you dive into the lessons, familiarize yourself with the lesson objectives. Then read the Scripture passages.

- Study them as a background to the lessons.
- Use them as a basis for your personal devotions.
- Think about how they relate to adults' circumstances today.

LESSON 1: KNOW WHAT YOU BELIEVE

Lesson Aim: To learn that, before we can share our faith with others, we must know what we believe—and what we don't yet understand.
Bible Basis: 1 Corinthians 15:1-11.

LESSON 2: THE VOICE OF EXPERIENCE

Lesson Aim: To discover that it's important to speak from experience and in plain language when telling someone about Christ.
Bible Basis: Acts 8:26-39 and Acts 17:22-34.

LESSON 3: ACTIONS SPEAK LOUDER

Lesson Aim: To learn how our actions can be a powerful witness for Christ.
Bible Basis: James 2:14-26; 1 Timothy 4:12; and Titus 2:6-8.

LESSON 4: I'LL DO IT MY WAY

Lesson Aim: To discover how we can each use our unique gifts and abilities to fulfill Christ's great commission to teach the nations.
Bible Basis: Matthew 28:18-20; Romans 12:3-8; and 1 Peter 4:7-11.

Publicity Page

Grab your congregation members' attention! Photocopy this page, then cut out and paste the clip art of your choice in your church bulletin or newsletter to advertise this course on evangelism. Or photocopy and use the ready-made flier as a bulletin insert. Permission to photocopy this clip art is granted for local church use.

Splash the clip art on posters, fliers, or even postcards! Just add the vital details: the date and time the course begins and where you'll meet.

It's that simple.

EVANGELISM
For Every Day

EVANGELISM
For Every Day

EVANGELISM
For Every Day

A 4-week adult course on sharing your faith in everyday circumstances

Come to _____

On _____

At _____

Come explore how you can fulfill the Great Commission to share God's love with the nations.

Know What You Believe

Finally, after months of prayer, your non-Christian friend approaches you at work and says, "You're a Christian, right? Well, what do you think about what's happenin' in the world? Where's God in all this mess?"

Your big opportunity has arrived! God has opened wide the door to your co-worker's heart. You sense that your co-worker is searching for something—for Someone. You open your mouth to let God's wonderful words of truth spill out and send this man to his knees in repentance. And...

...you don't know what to say. Come to think of it, you don't know what *you* believe.

This lesson will help the members of your class explore their beliefs so they can speak to others confidently about their faith.

OBJECTIVES

Participants will
- explore personal beliefs on significant theological issues;
- determine what's important to know about faith when telling someone about Christ; and
- learn that faith is a process, not a goal.

BIBLE BASIS

Look up the following Scripture. Then read the background paragraphs to see how the passage relates to adults today.

In **1 Corinthians 15:1-11,** Paul defines the importance of the Resurrection.

In these few verses, Paul sums up the main issues regarding our Christian faith. Paul emphasizes Jesus' post-resurrection appearances to the disciples and others to point to the fact that Jesus is indeed alive today. He reminds his readers that if Christ had not risen from the grave, their belief in Jesus would be in vain.

Paul, having once been a zealous persecutor of Christians, now worked hard to share God's message of love with his world. In verses 9-10, Paul introduces another important issue of the faith: He explains that he worked hard to grow in faith, yet it was God's grace that brought him along.

These verses point out the most significant issues Christians must understand before they can tell others about Christ. First, we must believe that Christ died for our sins, he was buried, and he rose from the

THE POINT

▶ BEFORE WE CAN SHARE OUR FAITH WITH OTHERS, WE MUST KNOW WHAT WE BELIEVE—AND WHAT WE DON'T YET UNDERSTAND.

1 CORINTHIANS 15:1-11

dead. Second, we must know that God's grace is a gift—we can't win it by doing good works. Paul knew this and wrote about it often in his letters. And finally, we must learn from Paul's example that we must give our all to grow closer to God and do God's work.

With these basic beliefs as a foundation, we can begin to unravel the rest of faith's mysteries through studying the Scriptures.

THIS LESSON AT A GLANCE

SECTION	MINUTES	WHAT PARTICIPANTS WILL DO	SUPPLIES
Welcome	1 to 3	Learn about today's lesson.	
Community Builder	5 to 10	**Option 1: My Biggest Question**—Tell each other what they don't understand about Christianity.	
	10 to 15	**Option 2: Faith Stories**—Share stories of how they became Christians.	
Bible Exploration and Application	10 to 15	**Option 1: Say What?**—Try to communicate something they don't fully understand.	Bibles
	20 to 25	**Option 2: What Are the Basics?**—Study basic issues of the Christian faith and determine what they believe about them.	Bibles, "What's Important?" handouts (p. 17), pencils
	10 to 15	**Option 3: Critical Issues**—Determine theological issues critical to their faith.	"Critical Issues" handouts (p.18), pencils
Closing	up to 5	**Option 1: Help Me to Know You**—Pray for confidence in reaching out to others.	
	up to 5	**Option 2: Guide Us**—Ask God to guide them in the coming weeks.	

The Lesson

WELCOME
(1 to 3 minutes)

As you begin the class, thank class members for attending and tell them what they'll be discussing in today's lesson. Use the following statement or your own summary of the main point: **Welcome to the first week of four on the topic of evangelism. In this study, we're going to explore how we can follow Christ's commandment to share God's love with the world.**

Not everyone is a skilled preacher or what we commonly call an "evangelist." But we're each called to share God's love. This course is designed to help us learn how to share our faith through our daily lives—not from a pulpit. We'll explore how the way we talk influences people's perceptions of the Christian faith, how our actions can speak louder than our words, and how each person here has a unique way to tell others about Christ.

THE POINT ▶

▶ Before we share our faith, however, we need to know what we believe—and what we don't fully understand about the Christian faith. That's where we'll begin today.

Encourage class members to get involved in the discussions and activities during the study.

OPTION 1: My Biggest Question
(5 to 10 minutes)

Form groups of four. Have the person in each group who's attended church the longest complete the following sentence: "The one thing I understand least about the Christian faith is..."

Have adults take turns telling what they don't understand about the Christian faith, then discuss the following questions. Ask the questions one at a time, allowing adults to discuss them before asking volunteers to share their groups' ideas with the whole class.

Ask:

● **Why are there so many mysteries in the Christian faith?** (The Bible is full of things that are hard to understand; God is bigger than our perceptions.)

● **How can we share our beliefs with others if we don't fully understand our faith?** (We can share what we know; we can be honest and say that we live by faith in many issues.)

● **What role does the Holy Spirit play in guiding us through the things we don't understand about the faith?** (The Holy Spirit guides us to truth even when we don't know where to go; the Holy Spirit gives us wisdom to know what's right.)

Say: ▶ **For us to be effective everyday evangelists, we must know the basics of our faith—that Christ died for our sins and that God desires that we take up our crosses and follow Christ. But we must also be honest and admit what we don't know about our faith.**

Christianity has been given a bad name in our media-saturated society. Yet when we're confident about the basics of faith and honest about the mysteries, non-Christians will discover the integrity of the Christian faith.

 OPTION 2: Faith Stories
(10 to 15 minutes)

Form groups of no more than four. Have adults each take no more than two minutes to tell their group how they became Christians.

After each adult has shared, have volunteers tell the whole group about some of their group members' stories. Draw out the diversity of experience in the group. Then ask the following questions and have adults discuss them in their groups:

● **What similarities are there in these faith stories?** (We all felt the need to reach out to God; God used other people to help us discover Christ.)

● **What roles did other Christians play in your faith journey?** (They led me to Christ; they helped me to see the need for a Savior; they showed me by example how wonderful it is to be a Christian.)

Say: **Whether it's a father who prays with his children or a friend who presents the Christian life by example, Christians can have a powerful influence on non-Christians. But how do we share our faith? What do we say?** ▶ **This lesson will help us discover that we need to know what we believe—and what we don't yet understand about our faith—before we share that faith with others.**

COMMUNITY BUILDER

◀ THE POINT

TEACHER TIP

People have wonderfully varied faith stories. Remind adults that some stories will be dramatic and dynamic ("I was rescued from drugs," or "I was an atheist until I saw a vision of Christ"). Others will be quiet and subtle ("I was raised in a Christian home," or "My faith journey began as a child, and I'm still on the road"). Both kinds of faith stories are equally valid and help us discover the incredible diversity and creativity of our faith.

If some class members aren't Christians or don't wish to tell their stories, allow them to pass or tell about a friend's faith journey.

◀ THE POINT

BIBLE EXPLORATION AND APPLICATION

TEACHER TIP

Adults may squirm a bit at this activity and wonder if they can answer the questions at all. Encourage them to do their best, as this feeling of inadequacy is the activity's goal.

 OPTION 1: Say What?
(10 to 15 minutes)

Have adults stay in their original groups of four and number off from one to four. Then assign the following questions to the appropriate group members.

Ones: **Why do bad things happen to good people and good things happen to bad people?**

Twos: **How can God be both just and merciful?**

Threes: **Are there physical boundaries to our universe? If so, what's outside of it?**

Fours: **In practical terms, how could Jesus have been fully human and fully God?**

Say: **Beginning with the ones, take no more than two minutes each to explain, as best you can, how you'd answer the question you've been assigned. You get bonus points if you can find or quote Scripture to support your answers. Ready, go.**

After about eight minutes, call adults together and have them stand. Ask the following questions one at a time. After asking a question, have volunteers share their answers, then sit down. People who would've answered the same way as the person who just spoke may also sit. Continue until everyone is seated for each of the questions.

Ask:

● **What was it like to answer these questions?** (I didn't know what to say; I'm not sure what I believe, so I couldn't answer my question.)

● **How is this experience like or unlike the way Christians communicate when talking to non-Christians about their faith?** (Sometimes we get caught up in theological issues that don't matter; we don't always know what we're talking about; the non-Christians ask unanswerable questions.)

● **Why is it important to know what you don't understand about the faith when talking with non-Christians?** (So they don't get the wrong message; so they know Christians aren't perfect; so you can be honest.)

● **What role does the Holy Spirit play when we tell others about Christ?** (The Holy Spirit leads the person to understanding; the Holy Spirit helps us speak the right words.)

● **What questions *should* we know the answers to when talking with non-Christians about our faith?** (What does it mean to be a Christian? How do you become a Christian? Who is Jesus Christ?)

Have a volunteer read aloud 1 Corinthians 15:1-11. Then have adults return to their groups of four to discuss the importance of these verses in telling others about Christ.

Allow a few minutes for discussion, then have volunteers tell what their groups discussed. Say: **When Paul wrote these words, he** **THE POINT ▶** **defined the essence of what Christians believe. ▶ We must know these basics and what we believe about other issues before we can effectively tell others about Christ.**

OPTION 2: What Are the Basics?
(20 to 25 minutes)

If you didn't use the previous activity, have groups of four number off from one to four.

Have the ones, twos, threes, and fours go to different corners of the room for the next part of this study. Say: **For the next 10 minutes, we're going to examine what we believe about significant theological issues.**

Give a Bible, a pencil, and a photocopy of the appropriate section of the "What's Important?" handout (p. 17) to each group member. Tell the class to follow the instructions on the handout.

After 10 minutes, call time and have adults re-form their original groups of four and share what they learned in the numbered groups. Then have volunteers share insights with the whole class.

Ask:

● **Which of these faith issues are most important to understand when talking with a non-Christian about faith in Christ?** (We need to know Jesus died for our sins; we need to know that Christianity is a lifestyle decision; we need to recognize the issues we don't understand.)

Say: **Obviously, we can't explore all sides of each theological issue in the short time we have in class.** ▶ **But we can begin to wrestle with the basics because we need to know what we believe before we can share our faith effectively. We're going to take the next few minutes to identify how critical some of these issues are to our faith.**

◀ THE POINT

 OPTION 3: Critical Issues
(10 to 15 minutes)

Give each person a copy of the "Critical Issues" handout (p. 18) and a pencil. Say: **Take the next five minutes to complete the handout, then choose a partner to discuss the questions at the bottom of the handout. Be honest about *your* beliefs and sensitive to *others'* beliefs as you discuss these issues.**

Allow 10 to 12 minutes for adults to complete the handout and discuss the questions at the bottom of the handout. Then have pairs pair up to form foursomes. Have adults take turns completing the sentence below, then discussing each other's answers. Have volunteers share their group members' ideas with the whole class.

Have adults complete the following sentence: ▶ **Before we share our faith with others, we must know what we believe because...**

Say: **Knowing what we believe also means knowing what we don't yet understand. It's OK not to have all the answers. When we're honest and tell a searching non-Christian that we don't fully understand what it means to be a Christian, we help that person see that faith isn't something you arrive at; rather, it is an ever-changing and growing relationship with God.**

Telling someone about your faith in Christ is more than simply saying the right words. In the upcoming sessions, we'll explore how to speak out of our faith experience, live out our faith, and develop our own styles of sharing Christ's love. Since this is a journey we take together, take the next few minutes to go around

◀ THE POINT

the room and encourage one another to be bold and courageous during this course and beyond. Let's take the next minute or so to build each other up in love.

Have adults encourage one another with phrases such as "I know you can tell others about Christ," or "God be with you." Then call adults together for the closing activity.

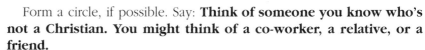

The "Digging Deeper" handout (p. 19) helps adults further explore the issues uncovered in today's class.

Give adults each a photocopy of the handout before they leave. Encourage them to take time out during the coming week to explore the questions and activities listed on the handout.

CLOSING

 OPTION 1: Help Me to Know You
(up to 5 minutes)

Form a circle, if possible. Say: **Think of someone you know who's not a Christian. You might think of a co-worker, a relative, or a friend.**

I'll open our prayer, then pause for people each to call out the name of the person they're thinking of. If you don't want to call out the name, say, "My friend" or "Someone at work." I'll close the prayer when each person here has spoken.

Open the prayer with: **Dear God, thank you for sending your Son to die for us. ▶ Help us to be know what we believe as we reach out to those who don't know you...**

After the last name has been spoken, close the prayer and dismiss the class.

Thank adults for participating and encourage them to use the "Digging Deeper" handout during the coming week.

THE POINT ▶

IF YOU STILL HAVE TIME...

More Big Questions—Have adults call out or write their biggest faith questions. Then form groups to explore and discuss these questions. Remind adults that it's OK if they don't find an answer today.

THE POINT ▶

OPTION 2: Guide Us
(up to 5 minutes)

Form groups of no more than six. Have adults in each group choose how they'd like to close the lesson. For example, groups might choose a time of silent prayer, or they might have one person pray for the whole group. Encourage adults to focus their prayer time on the main point of the class: ▶ Before we share our faith with others, we must know what we believe—and what we don't yet understand. And have adults ask God for guidance in the coming weeks as they explore how to be everyday evangelists.

Thank adults for attending and encourage them to use the "Digging Deeper" handout during the coming week.

WHAT'S IMPORTANT?

WHAT'S IMPORTANT:

Ones: What must we understand about the Bible before we can tell others about its significance for our faith?

Read the following Scripture passages. Discuss what they say about the inspiration of the Scriptures and what that means for you and the people you share your faith with.

2 Timothy 3:16-17; Romans 3:1-2; 1 John 5:9-12; Matthew 5:17; 1 Peter 1:10-12.

WHAT'S IMPORTANT:

Twos: What must we understand about God before we can tell others about our faith?

Read the following Scripture passages. Discuss what they say about God and what that means for you and the people you share your faith with.

Romans 1:18-20; Psalm 19:1; John 4:21-24; Deuteronomy 6:4-6; Acts 17:28-31; Psalm 139:7-12; Ephesians 2:4-5; 1 John 1:5.

WHAT'S IMPORTANT:

Threes: What must we understand about Jesus before we can tell others about our faith?

Read the following Scripture passages. Discuss what they say about Jesus and what that means for you and the people you share your faith with.

Isaiah 7:14; Galatians 4:4-5; Matthew 4:1-11; John 14:23; Mark 15:1-5; 1 Timothy 2:5-6; Romans 5:8; John 20:10-18.

WHAT'S IMPORTANT:

Fours: What must we understand about the Holy Spirit before we can tell others about our faith?

Read the following Scripture passages. Discuss what they say about the Holy Spirit and what that means for you and the people you share your faith with.

1 Corinthians 2:10-11; 2 Peter 1:21; John 14:16-17; Romans 8:26-27; 1 Corinthians 6:19; 1 Corinthians 12:13; Acts 2:1-4; John 16:12-15.

CRITICAL ISSUES

Read the following belief statements and determine how critical they are for your faith. If your faith depends on this truth, mark the "ultimately critical" box. If you believe the statement is true and would be surprised to find out it isn't, mark the "I believe it's true" box. If you believe the statement is true but wouldn't be surprised to find out you're wrong, mark the "I think it's true" box. And, if you're not sure what you believe about the issue, and it's not critical to your faith, mark the "I'm not sure" box.

	Ultimately Critical	I Believe It's True	I Think It's True	I'm Not Sure
Jesus is God's Son.	❑	❑	❑	❑
The Bible is the unerring Word of God.	❑	❑	❑	❑
Jonah was swallowed by a large fish.	❑	❑	❑	❑
God will bless those who love him.	❑	❑	❑	❑
Jesus walked on water.	❑	❑	❑	❑
Jesus died on the cross.	❑	❑	❑	❑
The Bible has answers to all of life's questions.	❑	❑	❑	❑
Jesus rose from the dead.	❑	❑	❑	❑
Jesus turned water into wine.	❑	❑	❑	❑
We were created to live in relationship with God.	❑	❑	❑	❑
Moses parted the Red Sea.	❑	❑	❑	❑
All good people will go to heaven.	❑	❑	❑	❑
The end of the world will come just as it's described in Revelation.	❑	❑	❑	❑

DISCUSSION QUESTIONS

• How easy was it for you to complete this handout?

• What role does faith play in understanding what it means to be a Christian?

• How can we grow in Christian wisdom?

Reflecting on God's Word

Each day this week, read one of the following Bible passages and examine what the passage means to your faith. You may want to list your discoveries in the space next to each Scripture reference.

Day One: Ephesians 3:12

Day Two: 1 Corinthians 12:5-28

Day Three: John 11:25-26

Day Four: Matthew 8:26

Day Five: Psalm 118:8

Day Six: John 3:16

Beyond Reflection...

1. Get a notebook and begin writing your statement of faith. List what you believe is most important for Christians to believe and what isn't as critical. Periodically, go back to your notebook and write new insights. You might want to discuss your faith journal with a friend.

2. Talk with other church members about their faith journeys. Ask for their greatest insights into the life of faith.

3. If you haven't already done so, make a plan to read through the entire Bible. Many study Bibles have plans for doing this. To make your experience more meaningful, meet with two or three other adults to discuss your findings once a week or so.

DIGGING DEEPER

THE LESSON
Know What You Believe

THE POINT
▶ BEFORE WE CAN SHARE OUR FAITH WITH OTHERS, WE MUST KNOW WHAT WE BELIEVE—AND WHAT WE DON'T YET UNDERSTAND.

SCRIPTURE FOCUS
1 CORINTHIANS 15:1-11

The Voice of Experience

Imagine you're sitting alone when a stranger walks up and begins to talk to you. The stranger says, "If you only flarfen with your whole heart, you'll become a stargle smippet and be saved from perpetual quigglesnurf."

Would you be confused? Sure. And that's the way some people might feel if you spoke the foreign language called Christianese when telling them about Christ.

This lesson will help adults see the importance of speaking plainly when talking about faith.

OBJECTIVES

Participants will
- discover the importance of speaking plainly about their faith,
- practice telling someone what it means to be a Christian, and
- explore how Paul and Philip taught others about Christ.

BIBLE BASIS

Look up the following Scriptures. Then read the background paragraphs to see how the passages relate to adults today.

In **Acts 8:26-39,** Philip is led by the Holy Spirit to speak to an Ethiopian.

The Ethiopians were one of the meanest nations of the time. But this particular Ethiopian was a Gentile student of the Jewish faith. It's likely that he had just spent time in Jerusalem to observe the recent Jewish feast of Pentecost. On his return trip, the Ethiopian paused to read from the book of Isaiah. Philip followed the lead of the Holy Spirit and was able to tell the Ethiopian about Jesus.

This story is significant for many reasons. First, it's significant that Philip followed the Holy Spirit's direction without question. Philip's example of obedience can be a model to all Christians who feel drawn to reach out to others.

Second, Philip knew where the Ethiopian was in his understanding of Scripture and began from that point in his teaching. All too often, we assume everyone else knows what we know, and we fail to communicate God's love because we speak outside of the other person's experience. Philip knew that the Ethiopian was studying a passage in Isaiah, and he began his discussion by talking about that passage.

Finally, Philip spoke in clear language and from his own experience to help the Ethiopian understand the good news about Jesus. Philip led

THE POINT

▶ IT'S IMPORTANT TO SPEAK FROM EXPERIENCE AND IN PLAIN LANGUAGE WHEN TELLING SOMEONE ABOUT CHRIST.

ACTS 8:26-39
ACTS 17:22-34

the man from a point of confusion or misunderstanding to a place of understanding and faith. Our goal, as Christians, should be to do the same—to help people understand the message of Christ so they, too, can choose to follow God.

In **Acts 17:22-34**, Paul preaches the good news in Athens.

Paul's message in this passage was directed to a group of nonbelievers rather than his more typical Jewish audience. Instead of directing the people to see God's prophesies fulfilled (as he would have preached to the Jews), Paul focused his message on the providence of a known God.

It's ironic that the Greeks thought an unknown god watched over Athens, the center of Greek wisdom. But Paul knew that the people really needed to discover the *known* God. Paul spoke to the people on their own level—fully aware of their beliefs and clearly explaining God's providence in terms they could understand.

It's appropriate to notice that not everyone listened to Paul and chose to follow God. Some even sneered. That's also true today. Yet, by speaking clearly and from our own experience of faith, we can open the door to Christ for the people we work with, live with, or meet on the street.

THIS LESSON AT A GLANCE

SECTION	MINUTES	WHAT PARTICIPANTS WILL DO	SUPPLIES
Welcome	1 to 3	Learn about today's lesson.	
Community Builder	5 to 10	**Option 1: Strange Worlds**—Share times they felt like strangers in a strange land.	
	5 to 10	**Option 2: What Does It Mean?**—Figure out a cryptic message.	
Bible Exploration and Application	10 to 15	**Option 1: Confuse Me**—Discover how difficult it can be to understand the language of faith.	Bibles, newsprint, marker, paper, pens
	15 to 20	**Option 2: Simple and True**—Study Acts 8:26-39 and 17:22-34 and practice telling one another what Christ means to them.	Bibles
	10 to 15	**Option 3: Real Life**—Brainstorm ways to share their faith in everyday situations.	Bibles, paper, pencils
Closing	up to 5	**Option 1: Simple Prayer**—Write a simple prayer to share with nonbelievers.	3×5 cards, pencils
	5 to 10	**Option 2: Confidence**—Describe times they told others about Christ.	

WELCOME
(1 to 3 minutes)

THE POINT ▶

The Lesson

As you begin the class, tell adults what you'll be learning in today's lesson. Use the following statement or your own summary of the main point: **Welcome to the second week of four on the topic of evangelism for every day. Last week we explored the importance of knowing what you believe.** ▶ **Today we're going to examine why it's important to speak from experience and in plain language**

when sharing your faith with someone.

Open with prayer. Encourage class members to get involved in the discussions and activities during the study.

 OPTION 1: Strange Worlds
(5 to 10 minutes)

Form trios. Have adults each tell a brief story about a time they felt like strangers or foreigners. Participants might tell about times they were in a foreign country or among people who spoke a different language. Encourage adults to focus on how they felt in those circumstances and what they learned from them.

Ask the following questions to help adults discuss these experiences:

● **What was it like to be a stranger in a strange land?** (I felt uncomfortable; I felt uneasy; I didn't know how to act.)

● **What was most uncomfortable for you?** (I didn't understand the language; I thought people didn't like me.)

● **How might the way you felt be like the way non-Christians feel in the midst of Christians?** (It's probably similar; when we talk about our faith, it probably seems foreign to non-Christians.)

● **How did you bridge the gap and overcome your feelings of being a foreigner?** (I learned to communicate; I became more accustomed to their language and customs.)

Say: **Too often we get so caught up in saying the right words or composing the right invitation for someone to know Christ that we ignore a strong ally—our own experience of faith. ▶ Today we're going to explore the importance of speaking plainly and from our own experience when sharing our faith.**

 OPTION 2: What Does It Mean?
(5 to 10 minutes)

Form groups of no more than four. Say: **I'm going to read a strange sentence to you, and you must work together to figure out what it really means. Work as a group to come up with your best guess. I'll divulge the true meaning after each group has guessed.**

Tell groups this sentence: **Frog sings his song today in a forest.** Give adults about three or four minutes to attempt to figure out the cryptic sentence. Then have a representative from each group tell the group's guess.

When all the groups have given their answers, tell them what the sentence really means: **God sent his Son to die for us.** Explain that the original message is simply an extremely bad pronunciation of the actual message. Then ask the following questions and have groups discuss them briefly before sharing their answers with the whole class.

Ask:

● **How did you attempt to figure out the meaning of the sentence?**

● **How did you respond when I told you the real meaning?** (I was confused; I didn't understand how you got that message.)

● **How was the cryptic message I gave you at first like the way many people hear the actual message you were trying to decipher?** (Christians often speak in language others don't understand; God's

◀ THE POINT

message is confusing to non-Christians until they accept Christ.)

Say: **While this exercise was an exaggeration, it's true that many non-Christians just don't understand what we're trying to say when we talk about our Christian faith.** ▶ **That's why it's important to speak in plain language and from our own experience when telling others about Christ. Let's take another look at what it's like to understand the language of faith.**

 OPTION 1: Confuse Me
(10 to 15 minutes)

Form two teams.

Say: **I'm going to give each team an odd message to share with the other team and a list of rules for sharing that message. After you've been given your instructions, take five minutes to discuss how you'll get the other team to understand your message.**

Call someone from each group aside one at a time and give each representative one of the following instructions:

Team 1: **You must communicate the following message without using any words (written or spoken). You may use facial expressions, hand motions, and other actions, but that's all. The message is: Three wise elephants know no more than one foolish ape.**

Team 2: **You must communicate the following message using only sounds (no words) and hand motions: Fine feathered friends often become fiends when framed.**

Give teams five minutes to discuss their strategies for communicating their messages. Then have each group present its message. Afterward, tell groups what the actual messages were and have them give each other a round of applause for their efforts.

Form groups of no more than four, mixing up members of both teams. Have adults answer the following questions and share their insights with the whole group.

Ask:

● **What was it like to try to communicate your message to the other group?** (Difficult; I wasn't quite sure how to do it; I felt ridiculous.)

● **How is that like or unlike how you feel when you tell someone about your faith?** (We're each a little unsure of how to tell someone about Christ; we each have different ideas about sharing our faith.)

● **How did you feel when you were trying to understand the other team's message?** (Frustrated; confused; I had no idea what the message was.)

● **How might that be like or unlike the way people feel when we tell them about Jesus?** (They don't hear what we're saying; the words sound like gibberish; even if they understand the words, they may not get the meaning.)

● **What are Christian words we use that non-Christians might not understand?** (Salvation; born-again; saved; reconciled.)

● **How does the use of this "Christianese" turn off non-Christians?** (They don't understand what it means; they feel uncomfortable with those words; they feel inferior because they don't know what the words mean.)

Have a volunteer in each group tell one meaningful faith experience in his or her life. For example, someone might tell about a time when he

THE POINT ▶

BIBLE EXPLORATION AND APPLICATION

TEACHER TIP

If your group is larger than 12, form four or six teams and pair them up according to the message they're to deliver. You may need to send teams to different corners of the room or adjoining rooms to allow teams to work on this activity at the same time.

or she felt especially close to God or a time when God answered a prayer. (This is a great way for people to "practice" sharing their faith.) After this brief story, have adults discuss the following questions and share insights with the whole class.

● **What are the differences between the way you received the message from the other team and the story told by your group member?** (One was important; one made sense; the team message was impossible to understand.)

● **How do the passion of our experience and the clarity of our speech affect how our words are understood?** (We can understand what people say when they talk about their experiences; we believe someone who speaks with passion.)

Say: **In this activity, the messages you tried to communicate were meaningless. The message of God's love is anything but meaningless—it's the most important message we can share with others. But when we talk about our faith, we sometimes talk a confusing language. And just as in this activity, people have a hard time understanding what we're saying. ▶ That's why it's important to speak plainly and from our own experience when telling others about our faith.**

 OPTION 2: Simple and True
(15 to 20 minutes)

Say: **Paul and Philip spoke in plain language when they talked about their faith. And they told of Christ's impact on their own lives.**

Form pairs. Assign one of the following passages to each person in the pair: Acts 8:26-39 (Philip) or Acts 17:22-34 (Paul). Say: **Read your assigned passage and briefly discuss how Philip and Paul communicated their faith to non-Christians. Then, using what you discover, take turns telling each other what being a Christian means to you. ▶ Don't search for the right Christian words to use, simply speak in plain language and out of your own faith experience. You have 10 minutes.**

After 10 minutes, have volunteers who studied each passage share their discoveries from the Scriptures and from practicing telling each other about what it means to be a Christian.

Ask:

● **How did Paul and Philip enter into discussions about Jesus?** (They took advantage of the moment; they knew about the other people's world and spoke to them in their own language.)

● **What's the most difficult thing to communicate when telling someone about Christ?** (What it really feels like to be a Christian; how much God loves us; that we don't know everything.)

● **What can we learn from Paul's and Philip's examples that can help us tell others about Christ?** (Listen to the Holy Spirit; help others understand the Scriptures; speak in clear language.)

Have partners thank each other for telling what being a Christian means to them. Encourage adults to give specific and meaningful affirmations to each other for opening up and being vulnerable in this activity.

◀ THE POINT

◀ THE POINT

 OPTION 3: Real Life
(10 to 15 minutes)

Have pairs pair up to form foursomes. Give each group a sheet of paper and a pencil. Say: **In your group, brainstorm the places and times you wish you could speak up about your faith. Think of real-life situations you experience. For example, if you wish you could talk about your faith with your boss or with family members, list that situation on your paper. Be specific about your group members' situations.**

THE POINT ▶

After about three minutes, call time. Say: ▶ **Now, starting with the first item on your list, use what you've already learned about speaking plainly and speaking from your faith experience. Discuss practical ways to tell that person or those people about Christ. You may want to refer to Acts 8:26-39 and 17:22-34 or any other verses for ideas on how to share your faith naturally.**

In seven minutes, I'll call time and ask you to share your ideas for specific situations.

After about seven minutes, call the class together and have volunteers report some of the groups' ideas for telling others about Christ in specific situations. Encourage new ideas from the rest of the class for each situation.

Say: **We don't need to pound people over the head with Christianese to help them understand the gospel. When we talk about our own faith experience, people catch a glimpse of our passion and love for Christ. And when we speak in terms others understand, people begin to learn what it means to be a Christian.**

 DIGGING

DEEPER

The "Digging Deeper" handout (p. 28) helps adults further explore the issues uncovered in today's class.

Give adults each a photocopy of the handout before they leave. Encourage them to take time out during the coming week to explore the questions and activities listed on the handout.

CLOSING

OPTION 1: Simple Prayer
(up to 5 minutes)

Have adults stay in their foursomes (or create new groups of four if you skipped the "Real Life" activity). Distribute 3×5 cards and pencils.

THE POINT ▶

Say: **In your group, compose a simple prayer you can share with a non-Christian who wants to become a Christian. ▶ Write your prayer on a 3×5 card and keep your card with you as a reminder to reach out to others by speaking plainly and from your own faith experience.**

Close the session by having adults pray in their groups for God to give them the right words when telling others about Christ.

OPTION 2: Confidence
(5 to 10 minutes)

To build participants' confidence, have volunteers describe for the whole class times they told others about Christ or what it means to be a Christian. Have adults briefly explain how they felt in the situation and what, if anything, has resulted.

Then have adults form small circles (of no more than four) for a closing prayer time. Before groups pray, have adults share concerns or needs they'd like the group to pray about. ▶ Remind adults to also pray for God to help them speak from experience and in plain language when telling others about Christ.

◀ **THE POINT**

IF YOU STILL HAVE TIME...

Defining Christianese—Have adults brainstorm a list of Christianese (words that have specific Christian meanings). Then have groups of no more than four each examine and define one or more of the words and share their findings with the whole class.

Another Country—Have adults brainstorm what it'd be like to take the gospel message to another country where people don't understand our language. Have groups of no more than four come up with ways to express that message without using words.

DIGGING DEEPER

THE LESSON
The Voice of Experience

THE POINT

▶ IT'S IMPORTANT TO SPEAK FROM EXPERIENCE AND IN PLAIN LANGUAGE WHEN TELLING SOMEONE ABOUT CHRIST.

SCRIPTURE FOCUS
ACTS 8:26-39 AND ACTS 17:22-34

Reflecting on God's Word

Each day this week, read one of the following Bible passages. Learn how the person in the passage lived out or shared his faith. Think of how you might apply these ideas to your own everyday evangelism. You may want to list your discoveries in the space next to each Scripture reference.

Day One: Acts 3:11-26 (Peter)

Day Two: Acts 4:1-22 (Peter and John)

Day Three: Acts 9:26-31 (Paul)

Day Four: Acts 10:1-48 (Peter)

Day Five: Acts 14:8-18 (Paul and Barnabas)

Day Six: Acts 17:1-4 (Paul and Silas)

Quick Quote
"Preach the gospel at all times. If necessary, use words."
—St. Francis of Assisi

Beyond Reflection...

1. Read the entire book of Acts. Record your discoveries about how the apostles taught about the Lord. Meet with a friend to talk about how you can implement some of your discoveries in your own life.

2. Read chapter 24 of *The Body* by Charles Colson (Word Publishing) and discuss it with a group of friends. This chapter, called "Being His Witnesses," explores the role of evangelism in the church.

Actions Speak Louder

God calls Christians to reach out and teach Christ's love. But *telling* people about the Lord of love is just part of the job. Living out Jesus' teachings is often the best way to show God's love to others. When we serve others willingly and love them unconditionally, we teach them by example what Jesus is all about.

OBJECTIVES

Participants will
- serve one another,
- discover how to be patterns of Christ, and
- explore the impact they can have on others by living Christlike lives.

BIBLE BASIS

Look up the following Scriptures. Then read the background paragraphs to see how the passages relate to adults today.

In **James 2:14-26**, James defines faith and good works.

This passage may seem to contradict Paul's assertion in Romans 3:28 that we are justified by faith only and not by works. In the Romans passage, Paul describes what it means to be justified by faith before God. Paul spoke his message to people who believed following the law of Moses could buy them God's grace. These self-justifiers needed to hear that God's grace is *not* based on following the letter of the Law—that God's grace is a free gift.

James' audience was different, however. He aimed his words at believers who seemed content with a lifeless, inactive faith. That wasn't unlike what they associated with the Jewish tendency to follow the Law as opposed to living a new life of holiness. James describes a faith that's justified before people, not before God.

However you interpret this passage, the message is still true: Faith in Jesus compels us to reach out and actively serve those around us. To paraphrase James, a faith without the evidences of faith (our actions) is a lifeless faith. Yet an active faith can be the best witness of Christ's love. Being an everyday evangelist requires that we act on our faith every day.

In **1 Timothy 4:12 and Titus 2:6-8,** Paul encourages young people to be good examples of the faith.

Paul's messages to Timothy and Titus reminded the two new Christians of the importance of being consistent in both action and word.

THE POINT
▶OUR ACTIONS CAN BE A POWERFUL WITNESS FOR CHRIST.

JAMES 2:14-26
1 TIMOTHY 4:12
TITUS 2:6-8

The word "example" as used in these passages literally means a "pattern." Paul's words paint a wonderful picture for new and more experienced Christians alike—we're to be patterns of Christ.

Being a pattern of Jesus Christ means we must act as he would act. This is not only a challenge, but the most significant goal we can attain as Christians—to become like Christ.

THIS LESSON AT A GLANCE

SECTION	MINUTES	WHAT PARTICIPANTS WILL DO	SUPPLIES
Welcome	1 to 3	Learn about today's lesson.	
Community Builder	5 to 10	**Option 1: Actions**—Perform various actions and guess what they represent.	Paper, pencils
	5 to 10	**Option 2: When Someone Cared**—Tell of times they felt loved.	
Bible Exploration and Application	10 to 15	**Option 1: Talking With Our Actions**—Use actions to show one another they care.	Bibles, coffee supplies, tea bags, hot water, cups, sweet rolls or doughnuts, napkins
	25 to 35	**Option 2: Patterns of Christ**—Study Scripture passages about faith and discover how they can become patterns of Christ.	Bibles, Bible commentaries, concordances, "Person Patterns" handouts (p. 35), paper, scissors
	10 to 15	**Option 3: One Action**—Choose and commit to performing actions showing Christ's love in the coming week.	Bibles
Closing	up to 5	**Option 1: Action Prayer**—Show God their love for one another.	
	5 to 10	**Option 2: Love One Another**—Thank God for one another's lives of faith	

The Lesson

WELCOME
(1 to 3 minutes)

THE POINT ▶

As you begin the class, tell adults what you'll be learning in today's lesson. Use the following statement or your own summary of the main point: **Welcome to the third week of four on the topic of evangelism for every day.**

▶**Today we're going to explore how Christlike actions can speak volumes to non-Christians.**

Open with prayer. Encourage class members to get involved in the discussions and activities during the study.

COMMUNITY BUILDER

 OPTION 1: Actions
(5 to 10 minutes)

Form groups of no more than four. Give each adult a sheet of paper and a pencil. Have each group come up with an activity to portray service, such as washing a car, raking leaves, or helping someone across the street. Encourage participants to choose an action that might be difficult to guess. Tell them that they'll be performing these actions for the rest of the class and to include everyone in their group in their action.

After about three or four minutes, choose a group to go first to perform its action. Have the other adults describe on their paper what action they think is being presented. Don't let adults tell what they portray.

After each group has performed its action, have adults call out what act of service they think each group portrayed. Then have a representative from each group tell what the action really was.

Ask:

● **What made it easy or difficult to determine the actions in this activity?** (Some were very subtle; they all looked alike; we couldn't guess what they were holding.)

● **What do these actions, when done in real life, say about those who perform them?** (That the person cares for others; that the person wants to give something to others.)

● **Which is a more powerful image to you: telling someone about the importance of serving others or actually serving someone? Explain.** (Serving others, because they reap the benefits and understand what serving means; telling others about serving, because they can think about what it means to them.)

Say: **In the past two lessons, we've explored how to tell others about our faith. ▶ But today, we're going to explore how our actions can be a powerful witness for Christ. We don't always have to speak the right words to teach someone about what it means to be a Christian. When we live Christlike lives, we show others who Jesus is. We don't just talk our faith, we walk it.**

 OPTION 2: When Someone Cared
(5 to 10 minutes)

Form groups of no more than four. Have adults take turns completing the following sentence: "One time I felt truly loved was…"

Have adults discuss the following questions after they each tell about a time they felt loved. Then gather adults together and have volunteers share insights from their discussions.

Ask:

● **What caused you to feel loved in the situation you described?** (Someone took an interest in me; someone helped me out when I was in need.)

● **What part did someone's words play in your situation?** (My friend talked to me when I was down; my friend shared encouraging words.)

● **What part did someone's actions play in your situation?** (My friend cooked supper for me; a friend gave me a hug when I needed it.)

Say: **Up to this point, we've been exploring the role of our words in reaching out to non-Christians. But as we've seen from these stories, our actions can speak volumes about love. ▶ Today we're going to explore how our actions can be a powerful witness for Christ.**

 OPTION 1: Talking With Our Actions
(10 to 15 minutes)

Place sweet rolls or doughnuts, napkins, and the materials necessary for making instant coffee and hot tea on a table.

◀ THE POINT

◀ THE POINT

BIBLE EXPLORATION AND APPLICATION

Say: **Since this lesson is about living our faith through our deeds, take the next seven minutes to let your actions do the talking to the people around you. Without saying a word, show your Christian love and service to the rest of the class.**

Say nothing more and watch how people react. If adults don't know what to do, set an example by serving coffee and a doughnut to someone. Another idea might be to give someone a hug or a back rub.

After about seven minutes, call adults together and have them form groups of no more than four. Encourage adults who haven't already gotten coffee or tea and a doughnut to do so now.

Ask the following questions and have adults take turns answering them in their groups. Then have volunteers tell the whole class what their groups discovered during the discussions.

Ask:

● **How did you feel when I first asked you to use your actions to show your Christian love and service?** (Embarrassed; unsure; confident.)

● **How is the way you acted when I gave this instruction like or unlike the way you act among non-Christian friends?** (I usually show others how I care for them; I don't usually serve others like this.)

● **What was it like to be served?** (It was fun; I enjoyed the attention.)

● **How does acting on our faith teach others about Christ?** (They see the way we act and want to know why; people are intrigued by someone who loves them unconditionally.)

Have someone read 1 Timothy 4:12 aloud. Say: **While this verse speaks specifically to those young in the faith, its message applies to all Christians. We're to live as examples through our words, actions, love, faith, and pure life. The word "example" is literally translated "pattern."** ▶ **Let's explore how we can be great witnesses for Christ by patterning our lives after his.**

THE POINT ▶

 OPTION 2: Patterns of Christ
(25 to 35 minutes)

Form groups of no more than five. Assign each group one of the following Scripture passages to study: 1 Timothy 4:11-16; Titus 2:6-8; 1 Peter 2:18-25; James 2:14-26. Provide New Testament Bible commentaries and concordances.

Say: **Read your passage, then discuss how this passage applies to our command to share the gospel with the whole world. You may use the commentaries to get a better handle on the passage. Or look up key words in a concordance to find Scripture passages with related themes. In 12 minutes, I'll call time and ask each group to report its findings.**

When time is up, have a volunteer from each group briefly summarize the passage the group studied and tell what the group learned about its meaning.

Then ask the following questions and encourage at least three different responses to each:

● **Why is it important to live out our faith through our actions?** (Because faith compels us to act; because God wants us to live what we believe.)

Say: **The word "example" in these passages means "pattern."**

As you talk, pass out paper, scissors, and cutouts from the "Person Patterns" handout (p. 35). Have adults try to cut or tear new shapes by following the patterns. Tell participants they may not trace the pattern, but must cut or tear their paper into the shapes simply by looking at the patterns they've been given.

If you don't have many scissors, that's OK. Encourage people to tear rather than cut. This can add to the discussion about following a pattern.

After everyone's created a paper person from a pattern, ask:

● **What makes following a pattern easy or difficult?** (If it's too intricate, it's too hard to follow; following a pattern doesn't require creativity.)

● **How is this activity like or unlike being a pattern of Christ?** (A lot easier; each person has to do it on his or her own.)

● **Based on what we read earlier, how can we become patterns of Christ?** (By demonstrating our faith; by showing compassion; by being consistent.)

Encourage adults to write these answers on their cutouts.

Ask:

● ▶ **How can our actions be a witness for Christ?** (When people experience God's love through someone, they want to know more about that love; our examples give other people something positive to look up to.)

◀ THE POINT

Say: **The way we live is one of the loudest things we do. To the people around us, our actions say a lot more than our words. That's why it's so important to be consistent in our actions and live our lives in a way that's pleasing to God.**

One way we live as a pattern for Christ is by showing each other the kind of love Christ shows us. Let's practice that by addressing at least three other people by completing the following sentence: "I see (or saw) a pattern of Christ in you when..." For example, you might say, "I see a pattern of Christ in you when you speak the truth boldly," or "I saw a pattern of Christ when you greeted everyone warmly in class today."

Join the group in affirming others. Look especially for people who might have been overlooked by other group members and affirm them.

 OPTION 3: One Action
(5 to 10 minutes)

Form pairs. Ask adults to read James 2:14-26. ▶ Then have each adult choose one thing to do this week to be a witness for Christ.

◀ THE POINT

Encourage adults to be specific about what they'll do. For example, someone might deliver cookies or a meal to a person who's recently been through a tough time. Or someone might offer to baby-sit so the parent(s) can have a free night.

Have adults make oral commitments to their partners to act on their ideas during the coming week.

After about five minutes, get adults' attention. Say: **Today's lesson reminds us that being a living witness for Christ is just as important as *telling* others what we believe. Let's commit together to become patterns for Christ as we reach out in Christian love to those around us.**

The "Digging Deeper" handout (p. 36) helps adults further explore the issues uncovered in today's class.

Give adults each a photocopy of the handout before they leave. Encourage them to take time out during the coming week to explore the questions and activities listed on the handout.

CLOSING

THE POINT ▶

OPTION 1: Action Prayer
(up to 5 minutes)

Say: ▶ **As a fitting closing prayer for this lesson, let's practice letting our actions show our witness for Christ by giving at least three other people a hug, a hearty handshake, or a pat on the back. Let these acts of Christian love be our prayer of thanks to God for giving us the desire and ability to share Jesus with those around us.**

Join the hugs or handshakes, then dismiss the class. Thank everyone for participating.

OPTION 2: Love One Another
(5 to 10 minutes)

Form trios. Beginning with the person nearest you, have each person in a trio complete the following prayer for the person on his or her left: "Dear God, thank you for (name) and (his or her) life of faith. Help (him or her) to always be an example of your love."

When adults have finished praying, close with this benediction: ▶ **May God be with us as we strive to live each aspect of our lives—our words, our actions, our love—as a witness for Christ.**

Thank everyone for participating.

THE POINT ▶

IF YOU STILL HAVE TIME...

Faith in Action—Have adults brainstorm ways they can, as a group, reach out in Christian love to non-Christians in your community. For example, they might plan a barbecue picnic for people in the church neighborhood or serve others by painting or fixing up someone's home.

James and Paul—Have adults study the similarities and differences in the messages given by Paul in Romans 3:28 and James in James 2:14. If possible, provide Bible commentaries to help adults explore the passages and their contexts.

PERSON PATTERNS

Cut out these shapes of people to provide patterns for each class member. Copy as many as you'll need. Repeats are OK.

DIGGING DEEPER

THE LESSON
Actions Speak Louder

THE POINT
▶ OUR ACTIONS CAN BE A POWERFUL WITNESS FOR CHRIST.

SCRIPTURE FOCUS
JAMES 2:14-26;
1 TIMOTHY 4:12; AND
TITUS 2:6-8

Reflecting on God's Word

Each day this week, read one of the following Bible passages and examine what it says to you about acting in love toward non-Christians. You may want to list your discoveries in the space next to each Scripture reference.

Day One: John 13:34

Day Two: Leviticus 19:34

Day Three: Ephesians 5:2

Day Four: Proverbs 15

Day Five: Proverbs 24

Day Six: Romans 12:3

Beyond Reflection...

1. Look for opportunities to put your faith into action in your community. For example, you might help out at a shelter for the homeless; sponsor a fun, yet meaningful event for neighborhood children; or visit people in a nursing home or detention center. As you put your faith into action, remember to focus on what you can give to others without expecting anything in return.

2. Ask your closest friends to rate how well you exemplify Christ in your life. Be prepared for less-than-perfect ratings, and ask your friends to be honest about what you could improve. Then pray together for wisdom to be more Christlike. Read Ephesians 4:17-32 as a discussion starter about what a life of faith should be like. Then take the ideas you discover and put them into practice.

I'll Do It My Way

"But I just don't feel comfortable talking about my faith." Sound familiar? Many Christians just aren't sure they're cut out to fulfill Christ's command to go to the ends of the earth—at least not as preachers or public teachers. But each Christian is called to teach the good news in some way. This lesson will help adults discover how they can use their God-given gifts and abilities to share the good news of Jesus Christ.

OBJECTIVES

Participants will
- explore their gifts and abilities,
- determine how they can follow Christ's command to share the gospel, and
- learn what kind of everyday evangelist they're most like.

BIBLE BASIS

Look up the following Scriptures. Then read the background paragraphs to see how the passages relate to adults today.

In **Matthew 28:18-20,** Jesus commands his disciples to teach all nations.

This familiar passage is often called the Great Commission. It's Jesus' final earthly speech to his apostles, yet it also carries significance for Christians today. The Great Commission is more than a command, it's a powerful encouragement to the apostles and their successors.

Jesus' command to teach others about God's love reminds us that we're to train people not only in creed, but in conduct. By our own actions and words, we're to show new Christians what it means to be Christlike. Thankfully, we're not alone in this monumental task. Jesus promises to be with us until the end of the age.

People often use this passage to support the idea of missionaries preaching around the world. But there's also a second, teaching flavor in the passage. All Christians can fulfill this command through their own gifts and abilities. This is Christ's command for us to be everyday evangelists—to teach others about God's love.

Romans 12:3-8 and **1 Peter 4:7-11** describe the diversity of gifts within the body of believers.

Both of these passages suggest that each person's gifts and abilities are

THE POINT

▶ WE CAN EACH USE OUR UNIQUE GIFTS AND ABILITIES TO FULFILL CHRIST'S GREAT COMMISSION TO TEACH THE NATIONS.

MATTHEW 28:18-20
ROMANS 12:3-8
1 PETER 4:7-11

equally important to the body of Christ. Both Paul and Peter also remind us that we're to use the gifts we've been given by God's grace and not let them stagnate.

In **1 Peter 4:11,** Peter encourages us to speak the pure word of God in our public and private ministries. And in **Romans 12:6,** Paul encourages us to use and develop our gifts.

When we apply the diversity of talents and abilities we've been given to Jesus' command in the great commission, it's easy to see how each person can play a different role in sharing God's love with others.

THIS LESSON AT A GLANCE

SECTION	MINUTES	WHAT PARTICIPANTS WILL DO	SUPPLIES
Welcome	1 to 3	Learn about today's lesson.	
Community Builder	10 to 20	**Option 1: Diversity**—Discover similarities and differences among themselves.	Paper, marker, tape
	10 to 15	**Option 2: I'm Unsure**—Explore their fears of telling others about Christ.	Newsprint, marker
Bible Exploration and Application	10 to 15	**Option 1: Every Which Way**—Discover how each person has a unique perspective.	"What Do You See?" hand-outs (p. 44), paper, pencils
	20 to 25	**Option 2: Finding Your Comfort Zone**—Explore Bible verses to discover what kind of everyday evangelism they can use to fulfill the Great Commission described in Matthew 28:18-20.	Bibles, "Everyday Evangelists" handouts (p. 45), pencils
	5 to 10	**Option 3: What I'll Do**—Form a support group for telling others about Christ.	"Everyday Evangelists" hand-outs (p. 45), pencils
Closing	up to 5	**Option 1: God Be With Us**—Pray for God's strength as they reach out to non-Christians.	
	up to 5	**Option 2: Thanks**—Thank one another for the support and wisdom they've shared.	

The Lesson

As you begin the class, tell adults what they'll be studying in today's lesson. Use the following statement or your own summary of the main point: **Welcome to the final week of our study on evangelism for every day. We've explored what it means to live out our faith, how to talk about our faith in plain language, and what we need to know to tell someone about Christ. ▶ Today we're going to see how we can each use our unique gifts and abilities to teach others about Christ. And we'll commit to using the gifts we've been given to share God's love with others.**

Open with prayer. Encourage class members to get involved in the discussions and activities during the study.

WELCOME
(1 to 3 minutes)

THE POINT ▶

OPTION 1: Diversity
(10 to 20 minutes)

At one end of the room, tape a sheet of paper with "1" written on it. Tape another paper with "2" on it at the other end of the room.

Say: **I'm going to read aloud several statements, then direct you to stand by the number representing the statement that best describes you. After you choose where you'll stand, quickly find a partner and tell that person why this statement describes you better than the other. There are no right or wrong answers.**

Read the following statements, allowing a minute or so between each pair of statements for participants to discuss why they chose that statement.

If you consider yourself an extrovert, stand by #1.
If you consider yourself an introvert, stand by #2.

If you enjoy helping other people through your actions, stand by #1.
If you enjoy helping other people through teaching or speaking, stand by #2.

If you're somewhat afraid of the thought of telling someone about your faith, stand by #1.
If you're invigorated by the thought of telling someone about your faith, stand by #2.

If you feel confident in your understanding of the basics of Scripture, stand by #1.
If you feel you need more training to comprehend the basics of Scripture, stand by #2.

If you're especially good with children, stand by #1.
If you're better among other adults, stand by #2.

If you're more like a lion, stand by #1.
If you're more like a duck, stand by #2.

Have ducks and lions form groups of no more than four with at least one duck and one lion in each group, if possible. Ask the following questions and, beginning with a lion in each group, have adults discuss them. Ask volunteers to share insights with the whole class.

Ask:
● **What conclusions can you draw from this exercise?** (This is a diverse group of people; we have a lot in common.)
● **What trends, if any, did you discover from this activity?** (All the extroverts enjoy public speaking; most of the extroverts considered themselves to be lions.)

Say: **This activity gives us a glimpse of the diversity of abilities and gifts in this group. ▶ As everyday evangelists, we can take advantage of this diversity to reach more people with God's message of love.**

◀ THE POINT

OPTION 2: I'm Unsure
(10 to 15 minutes)

Form pairs. Have partners take turns completing the following sentence: "The thing that scares me most about being an everyday evangelist is…"

Have adults discuss their fears for about three minutes, then have them call out their fears so you can list them on newsprint. Then have pairs pair up to form foursomes.

When you've completed the list, have adults refer to it and answer the following questions in their foursomes.

● **Based on this list, what conclusions can you draw about our fears?** (There are many different fears; we all have similar concerns.)

● **How might we overcome these fears so we can better tell others about Christ?** (Form support groups; trust God; work as a team.)

● **How does this list of fears reflect the diversity of gifts and abilities in our class?** (Some people are afraid of rejection; some people are afraid they won't have enough opportunities to share their faith; some people don't have many fears.)

Say: **Our fears often reflect our lack of confidence in certain areas such as public speaking or communicating clearly. But, as we said at the beginning of this course, not everyone has to be a great public speaker to be an everyday evangelist. ▶ Today we're going to explore how we can use our unique gifts and abilities to fulfill Christ's command to teach the nations.**

THE POINT ▶

BIBLE EXPLORATION AND APPLICATION

OPTION 1: Every Which Way
(10 to 15 minutes)

Form groups of no more than four. Give each person a sheet of paper and a pencil and give each group a photocopy of the "What Do You See?" handout (p. 44).

Say: **We're going to do a little variation on an inkblot test. Number your paper from one to four, then look at the handout and describe on your paper what you see in each of the four illustrations on the handout. Don't talk with anyone else about what you see.**

After about two minutes, call time and have adults share with their groups what they saw in each of the four pictures.

Then ask the following questions, allowing discussion time for each before having volunteers share their groups' insights with the whole class.

Ask:

● **What trends, if any, did you discover in the way people interpreted the pictures?** (Some people always saw animals; some people didn't see anything.)

● **How is diversity of perspectives in this activity like the diversity of perspectives in the world we live in?** (Each person sees things a little differently; some people believe that what they see is right.)

Have adults each point out how they saw what they did in the illustrations.

Ask:

● **How did your own view of the illustration change after hearing the other group members' descriptions?** (I began to see their ideas in the illustration; I saw more than one perspective; it didn't change my perspective at all.)

Say: **Just as each of us may have seen a different object in the illustrations, the non-Christians we interact with may have different perspectives on Christianity or what it means to be a Christian. Some may have no idea at all, others may be sure they have all the answers, and still others may be searching for truth without really knowing what it looks like.**

Have someone read aloud Matthew 28:18-20. Ask:

● **What does this passage tell us about who must share God's love with the world?** (Every Christian is responsible for telling others about Christ; the preachers and teachers are called to spread the gospel.)

● **How does this passage speak to you personally?** (It makes me nervous; I feel honored to be given such a responsibility.)

Say: **Because each person's needs and perspectives are different, we must use different methods to tell people about God's love. And that's where the diversity of our own gifts and abilities comes into play. ▶ Let's see how each person's gifts can help others discover God's love.**

◀ THE POINT

 OPTION 2: Finding Your Comfort Zone
(20 to 25 minutes)

Form groups of no more than four. Give each person a photocopy of the "Everyday Evangelists" handout (p. 45) and a pencil. Say: **Complete your handout to find out what kind of everyday evangelist you're most like. Then discuss the questions at the bottom of the handout with your group.**

Allow 10 to 15 minutes for adults to complete the handouts and discuss the questions. Then have adults share insights from their groups with the whole class.

Then say: **Each method for telling someone about Christ is valid. ▶Whether you're a public preacher or a subtle servant, your gifts can help fulfill the Great Commission.**

◀ THE POINT

Have adults tell the other members of their group what they most appreciate about their styles of everyday evangelism. For example, someone might tell a public preacher how much he or she appreciates the boldness of that person's witness. Or someone might tell a subtle servant how much he or she appreciates the time that person spends helping others.

 OPTION 3: What I'll Do
(5 to 10 minutes)

Have adults form groups of no more than four with representatives of at least two types of everyday evangelists (based on the "Everyday Evangelists" handout) in each group. If you skipped the "Finding Your Comfort Zone" activity, have adults first complete the "Everyday Evangelists" handout (p. 45) before continuing.

Have group members determine ways they'll support one another's everyday evangelism during the coming weeks. Have adults determine a plan of support that includes how long they'll be committed to helping each other, when (and if) they'll meet together, and what they'll do to encourage each other's talents and gifts. Encourage adults to be accountable to their group members during the agreed-upon time. Ask adults to write their plans on the back of their "Everyday Evangelists" handouts.

Say: **Write one another's names and phone numbers on your handouts. Do your best to support one another as you've planned.**

THE POINT ▶ ▶ **Together, with our unique abilities and gifts, we can help fulfill Christ's great commission to teach all the nations about God's love.**

The "Digging Deeper" handout (p. 46) helps adults further explore the issues uncovered in today's class.

Give adults each a photocopy of the handout before they leave. Encourage them to take time out during the coming week to explore the questions and activities listed on the handout.

CLOSING

 OPTION 1: God Be With Us
(up to 5 minutes)

Form a circle (or have adults stand as close together as possible). Have adults join you in a closing prayer. Open the prayer by saying:

THE POINT ▶ ▶ **Dear God, thank you for bringing us here today to discover our unique ways of sharing your love with others. Help us be everyday evangelists in all situations and with all people. Help us as we reach out...** Have adults continue the prayer by calling out times when they'll reach out to others with God's love or people they'll reach out to. For example, someone might continue the prayer by saying "to my co-workers" or "when I'm visiting my relatives" or "when someone asks me what I believe." Close the prayer by saying "amen," then thank everyone for participating in the course.

Ask adults what they liked most about the course as well as how they think it could be improved. Please note their comments (along with your own) and send them to the Adult Curriculum Editor at Group Publishing, Inc., Box 481, Loveland, Colorado 80539. We want your feedback so that we can make each course we publish better than the last. Thanks!

OPTION 2: Thanks
(up to 5 minutes)

Say: **In the past four lessons, we've explored how we can be evangelists in everyday situations. And today, we've made a commitment to use our unique talents and gifts to fulfill Christ's great commission to teach the nations about God's love.**

As a closing prayer, take the next few minutes to thank other people in class for their good ideas or encouragement. Use this time as a prayer of thanksgiving for the fellowship and support of fellow Christians wanting to do God's will.

After a few minutes, get adults' attention and thank each person specifically for his or her contribution to the course.

Ask adults what they liked most about the course as well as how they think it could be improved. Please note their comments (along with your own) and send them to the Adult Curriculum Editor at Group Publishing, Inc., Box 481, Loveland, Colorado 80539. We want your feedback so we can make each course we publish better than the last. Thanks!

IF YOU STILL HAVE TIME...

Review—Have adults form groups of no more than four to review the main points of the four lessons. Refer to the first pages of each lesson (pp. 11, 21, 29, and 37) for the points. Have adults describe what they learned that will help them be everyday evangelists in the days ahead.

Great Evangelists—Have adults brainstorm well-known examples of the public preacher type of evangelist (such as Billy Graham). Have adults discuss what they think of these people and their unique gifts of sharing the gospel. Have adults pray for those people gifted as preachers and the pastors of their own churches to speak God's truth boldly.

WHAT DO YOU SEE?

EVERYDAY EVANGELISTS

Use this handout to determine how you can best use your gifts to share God's love with others.

Read the descriptions below and determine which best fits your style of sharing Christ with others. It's likely that you fit more than one category, but determine which you fit the best, then mark that box.

❑ **TIMID TEACHER**—You enjoy one-on-one interaction about faith issues. You don't feel comfortable in front of a classroom of people, but you're perfectly comfortable sharing Scripture truths with someone who's approached you about the faith.

❑ **SUBTLE SERVANT**—While you don't feel comfortable talking about your faith, you live it out daily by opening your house to others, reaching out to those in need, and trying to live a Christlike life. You're the first one in line to prepare a meal for someone in need, but you would rather not speak during the worship service about your quiet witness for Christ.

❑ **PUBLIC PREACHER**—You're very comfortable speaking in front of people about God's love. You may not be a preacher by trade, but you are in practice. You believe your strength is understanding the Scriptures and helping people discover how the Bible applies to their lives.

❑ **AFFIRMING ANCHOR**—You spend much of your time supporting fellow Christians in their efforts. You don't feel called to preach to non-Christians, but rather to serve those who do. You're a born affirmer and love to encourage others.

❑ **OPPORTUNITY KNOCKER**—You don't feel comfortable bringing up your faith in conversations with non-Christians, but when an opportunity arises to share your faith with someone, you're not afraid to speak honestly.

❑ **BUTTON BLASTER**—You wouldn't be uncomfortable wearing a button or T-shirt proclaiming God's love. You enjoy publicly showing that you love God. You invite people to talk with you about what it means to be a Christian.

Once you've determined which type of everyday evangelist you're most like, read Romans 12:3-8 and 1 Peter 4:7-11 to see what Paul and Peter have to say to you about using your gifts.

Then discuss the following questions in your group:
- What gifts listed in Romans 12:3-8 and 1 Peter 4:7-11 match the various types of everyday evangelists listed on this handout?
- What do Paul and Peter have to say about using your gifts to proclaim God's truth?
- How does each style of everyday evangelism help people know Christ?
- How do the various types of everyday evangelism complement and support each other?
- Which everyday-evangelist traits would you like to develop further? How will you develop those traits?

DIGGING
DEEPER

THE LESSON
I'll Do It My Way

THE POINT
▶ WE CAN EACH USE OUR UNIQUE GIFTS AND ABILITIES TO FULFILL CHRIST'S GREAT COMMISSION TO TEACH THE NATIONS.

SCRIPTURE FOCUS
MATTHEW 28:18-20; ROMANS 12:3-8; AND 1 PETER 4:7-11

Reflecting on God's Word

Each day this week, read one of the following Bible passages and think about how it applies to your style of sharing the gospel. You may want to list your discoveries in the space next to each Scripture reference.

Day One: 2 Timothy 1:7

Day Two: Matthew 8:26

Day Three: Proverbs 3:5

Day Four: Matthew 5:42

Day Five: Proverbs 8:17

Day Six: 1 John 3:17

Beyond Reflection...

1. Invite a friend to watch a few TV evangelists at work. Then discuss what you observe and hear from the evangelists in light of what you've learned in this course. If you feel concerned about the methods used by one or more of these people, write a letter to that person stating your concerns. Be fair and loving as you explain your concerns.

If you appreciate something the evangelist says or does, write and tell that person.

2. Plan a time to meet informally with members of this course after a month or so has passed. Over coffee, discuss how things have changed in their everyday evangelism since the end of the course. Use this time to offer praise for positive things that have happened and encouragement for the days ahead.

COMMUNITY BUILDERS AND DISCUSSION STARTERS

In Your Face—Have adults interview Christians who feel the best way to share the gospel is through the "in your face" approach often used in street witnessing. Have adults explore the benefits and disadvantages of confronting unsuspecting people directly about their faith. Discuss how this approach is similar to and different from the way Jesus confronted people.

Across the Seas—Invite a retired missionary to speak to your class on the role of missionaries in spreading the gospel. Encourage adults to ask questions about the missionary's experiences—both positive and negative. Then have adults write encouraging notes to other missionaries from your church or denomination.

Church Questions—Have adults create a written (or phone) faith survey to present to friends, co-workers, and neighbors. Have adults include survey questions such as
- Do you believe in God? Why or why not?
- What is your perception of the church? the Bible?
- Who is Jesus Christ?
- What must a person do to get to heaven?

Have adults conduct the survey and meet to discuss the results.

Good News—Have adults develop a "Good News" newsletter or insert for your church newsletter telling positive stories about new Christians. The newsletter might include such column ideas as "Creative Ways to Share Your Faith at Work," "How to Reach Out to Someone in Need," and "Prayer Concerns."

For added benefit, have a pastor write a regular column on the basics of the Christian faith.

Altar Calls—Form a task force to explore the ways churches in your community approach the concept of altar calls (direct invitations during worship to people to accept Christ as their personal Lord and Savior). Have task force members present their findings and discuss their implications for your church. Discuss questions such as
- When does an altar call become manipulative?
- How can the Holy Spirit work through the altar call experience?
- Should a pastor always give an altar call? sometimes? never?

Church Visit—If your church is small or medium-sized, visit the nearest "mega-church" and examine its methods for reaching out to non-Christians. Arrange to talk with a pastor of evangelism about successful techniques for bringing more non-Christians to church. After your visit, discuss ideas for embracing more non-Christians into the fellowship of your church.

Digging Deeper—Use the "Digging Deeper" handouts (pp. 19, 28, 36, 46) as the basis for a meeting with adults. During the meeting, have adults review their handouts and discuss them. Ask participants to tell of times they told others about Christ—the successes as well as the disasters.

OUTREACH IDEAS

Door-to-Door—Take the more adventuresome members of your class on a door-to-door visit in your church neighborhood. Invite the people you meet to visit your church. Or, plan a special social event to introduce community members to your church and experience the fellowship of caring Christians.

Real Service—Have adults act on their faith by volunteering to help in your community. Check with local social-service agencies for the programs with the greatest need. Challenge adults to stretch themselves and give sacrificially to help with these programs. Plan to debrief the activities so adults can learn from one another's experiences.

Evangelism for the Year 2000—Have adults explore society's emerging trends. Research books and periodicals that describe what adults will be like in the year 2000 and beyond. Then have adults brainstorm ways the church will have to change to meet these people's needs. Based on changing morals, technology, and other trend factors, explore what evangelism will look like in the future.

PARTY IDEA

Free Food, No Pulpit Pounding—Have adults plan a monthly barbecue or other meal for community members with no church affiliations. Adults will need to prepare fliers announcing the event and perhaps even go door to door inviting people. Describe the meal as a gift to the people, with no strings attached.

Don't force people to sit through a sermon. Instead, make the simple connection that God's grace is free, like the meal, to any who choose to accept it. Invite interested people to talk with adults after the meal for more information on what it means to be a Christian. Invite them to future adult and children's classes at church.